How to Choose Your Tree

A Guide
to
Parklike
Landscaping
in Illinois,
Indiana,
and Ohio

By Dwight R. McCurdy,

William Greg Spangenberg,

and Charles Paul Doty

Southern Illinois University Press
Carbondale and Edwardsville

Feffer & Simons, Inc.
London and Amsterdam

Copyright © 1972 by Southern Illinois University Press
All rights reserved
Printed in the United States of America
Designed by Andor Braun
International Standard Book Number 0-8093-0514-3
Library of Congress Catalog Card Number 74-156791

Contents

Preface

The increasing demands being placed on our parks and recreation areas are creating a need for more intensive planning and management of the vegetation on the developed site. In many parks, use has become so heavy that it exceeds the vegetation's natural capacity to maintain and repair itself. For example, soil is compacted, roots are exposed, and trees are damaged on such areas as campgrounds and picnic areas. The end result is a park devoid of much of its natural charm.

Therefore, as use becomes heavy, planners and landscape architects must select vegetation that is both functional for the intended purpose and can survive and grow in a healthy manner. For example, there may be a need for a screen between units in a campground. Here, the planner might best select trees that grow relatively fast and produce dense foliage. However, the trees planted should also be able to withstand soil compaction, bumping by cars and trailers, chopping by little boys, and have many other desirable characteristics that would enhance the campers' experience.

In addition, the land managers must supplement a site's natural capacity to repair itself through applied management techniques. Treatments will need to be tailored not only to the use planned, but to the trees and their individual characteristics. A situation might warrant thinning a stand of trees to allow greater sunlight penetration which will increase ground vegetation and thereby make the site more durable. The degree to which the stand can be thinned will depend on the tree species present and their characteristics in such things as rooting patterns (windthrow), bark thickness (sunscald), and epicormic branching.

Therefore, this manual entails a synthesis of characteristics of fifty native trees that affect their suitability for the various uses to which they may be put and the silvicultural treatments that may be required in the parklike landscape in Illinois, Indiana, and Ohio. Only native trees were chosen because National Park and State Park policies dictate that only native trees be used within their boundaries. Parks within these systems are generally maintained, or where necessary, as nearly as possible, re-created in the condition that prevailed when the area was first visited by the white man.

PREFACE

The authors would like to express appreciation to A. G. Chapman, David T. Funk, John E. Krajicek, and Craig Losche of the U.S. Forest Service; to Neil W. Hosley and Paul L. Roth of the Forestry Department, Southern Illinois University at Carbondale; and to Leon S. Minckler of the Forestry Department at Syracuse University, New York, for contributing advice from their expertise as forest biologists.

The authors also wish to thank the McIntire-Stennis Cooperative Forestry Program, U.S. Department of Agriculture and the School of Agriculture, Southern Illinois University for sponsoring the research necessary in compiling this book. We would also like to acknowledge the help of the U.S. Forest Service, which provided most of the photographs used in illustrating the various tree characteristics.

How to use this manual

When selecting a tree to use on a parklike landscape, consideration might first be given to the purpose or purposes which it is to serve. For example, a tree may serve as shade, screen out undesirable sights, give scale and proportion to desired features, interrupt reflected light, or many other purposes. A second consideration might then be to select the tree species that have the characteristics to fulfill that purpose. These characteristics are described and synthesized in Part I. The characteristics of fifty native trees that thrive in Illinois, Indiana, and Ohio are summarized in table form at the end of each section. The third step would then be to determine which of the trees that have the required characteristics will survive and grow in a healthy manner on the planting site in question. The trees' site requirements are discussed and summarized in the tables in Part II. Upon finding that the desired tree species may not be compatible with the planting area, one might then determine if cultural treatments such as watering, draining, or fertilizing might partially overcome the site conditions which are limiting.

The fifty trees discussed in this book, and their scientific names, are:

Ash, Green	*Fraxinus pennsylvanica*
Ash, White	*Fraxinus americana*
Basswood, American (Linden)	*Tilia americana*
Beech, American	*Fagus grandifolia*
Birch, River	*Betula nigra*
Buckeye, Ohio	*Aesculus glabra*
Catalpa	*Catalpa speciosa*
Cedar, Eastern Red	*Juniperus virginiana*
Cherry, Black	*Prunus serotina*
Cottonwood, Eastern	*Populus deltoides*
Crab Apple	*Malus speciosa*
Cucumber Tree (Magnolia)	*Magnolia acuminata*
Dogwood, Flowering	*Cornus florida*
Elm, American	*Ulmus americana*
Elm, Slippery	*Ulmus rubra*
Gum, Black	*Nyssa sylvatica*

Gum, Sweet	*Liquidambar styraciflua*
Hackberry	*Celtis occidentalis*
Hawthorn	*Crataegus speciosa*
Hickory, Bitternut	*Carya cordiformis*
Hickory, Mockernut	*Carya tomentosa*
Hickory, Pignut	*Carya glabra*
Hickory, Shagbark	*Carya ovata*
Hickory, Shellbark	*Carya laciniosa*
Hornbeam, American	*Carpinus caroliniana*
Hornbeam, Hop	*Ostrya virginiana*
Locust, Black	*Robinia pseudoacacia*
Locust, Honey	*Gleditsia triacanthos*
Maple, Black	*Acer nigrum*
Maple, Red	*Acer rubrum*
Maple, Silver	*Acer saccharinum*
Maple, Sugar	*Acer saccharum*
Oak, Black	*Quercus velutina*
Oak, Bur	*Quercus macrocarpa*
Oak, Chinkapin	*Quercus muehlenbergii*
Oak, Northern Red	*Quercus rubra*
Oak, Pin	*Quercus palustris*
Oak, Post	*Quercus stellata*
Oak, Shingle	*Quercus imbricaria*
Oak, Swamp White	*Quercus bicolor*
Oak, White	*Quercus alba*
Osage Orange	*Maclura pomifera*
Persimmon	*Diospyros virginiana*
Pine, Eastern White	*Pinus strobus*
Poplar, Tulip (Yellow Poplar)	*Liriodendron tulipifera*
Redbud, Eastern	*Cercis canadensis*
Sassafras	*Sassafras albidum*
Sycamore	*Platanus occidentalis*
Walnut, Black	*Juglans nigra*
Willow, Black	*Salix nigra*

TREE CHARACTERISTICS

Shape of mature crown

Trees can provide many of the essential elements of beauty in a landscape, such as variety, harmony, contrast. They may also be used to delineate, frame, or conceal physical structures or unsightly areas. However, to do so the planner should know the form of plant materials, especially crown shape for trees. For example, trees with round crowns provide more shade or sun protection than oblong-shaped trees.

Six crown forms for mature, open-grown trees.

Figure 1

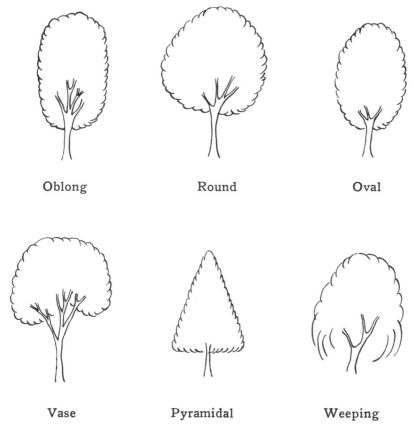

Oblong	Round	Oval

Vase	Pyramidal	Weeping

Pruning and trimming are often used to obtain and keep a desired form. However, this becomes difficult and expensive as the trees become larger.

Black Gum

Pignut Hickory

Shagbark Hickory

White Oak

Crab Apple

Bur Oak

Black Locust

American Basswood

Black Maple

Ohio Buckeye

Red Maple

Silver Maple

Eastern Cottonwood (summer)

Eastern Cottonwood (winter)

American Elm

Eastern White Pine

Pin Oak

River Birch

Black Willow

1. Open-grown crown shape of mature trees.

Tree species	Crown shape
Ash, Green	oval; oblong
Ash, White	oval
Basswood, American	round; oval; pyramidal; oblong
Beech, American	round; oval
Birch, River	weeping
Buckeye, Ohio	oval
Catalpa	oval
Cedar, Eastern Red	pyramidal
Cherry, Black	round; oblong
Cottonwood, Eastern	round; vase; oblong
Crab Apple	round
Cucumber Tree	pyramidal; oblong
Dogwood, Flowering	oval
Elm, American	vase
Elm, Slippery	vase
Gum, Black	oblong
Gum, Sweet	oblong
Hackberry	pyramidal
Hawthorn	round
Hickory, Bitternut	oblong
Hickory, Mockernut	oblong
Hickory, Pignut	oblong
Hickory, Shagbark	oblong
Hickory, Shellbark	oblong
Hornbeam, American	round
Hornbeam, Hop	round
Locust, Black	round; oblong
Locust, Honey	round; oblong
Maple, Black	round, oval
Maple, Red	oval
Maple, Silver	round; vase; weeping
Maple, Sugar	round; oval; oblong
Oak, Black	oval
Oak, Bur	round; oval
Oak, Chinkapin	round

SHAPE OF MATURE CROWN

Table 1. (*continued*)

Tree species	Crown shape
Oak, Northern Red	round
Oak, Pin	pyramidal
Oak, Post	oblong
Oak, Shingle	round
Oak, Swamp White	round
Oak, White	round
Osage Orange	round
Persimmon	round
Pine, Eastern White	pyramidal
Poplar, Tulip	oblong
Redbud, Eastern	round; oval
Sassafras	oval
Sycamore	round; oval; pyramidal
Walnut, Black	round; oblong
Willow, Black	weeping

Height

MATURE HEIGHT. Along with a tree's shape, its height is also an important dimensional characteristic. For example, tall trees placed beneath power lines, when mature will require frequent trimming which often severely modifies their shape. Another frequent mistake is planting trees which dominate (dwarf) the structure or building they are to beautify.

Five strata of tree height (at maturity) follows:

Very Small:	less than 30 feet
Small:	30 to 45 feet
Medium:	45 to 60 feet
Tall:	60 to 75 feet
Very Tall:	75 to 100 feet or more

GROWTH RATE. How rapidly the tree will reach its mature height is also important. When developing screening, foresters often plant less desirable, fast-growing trees in mixture with more desirable, slow-growing trees to provide a temporary screen. On the other hand, there are frequent situations where a slow-growing tree is preferred.

Three classes of height growth follow:

Slow:	1 foot of growth or less per year
Medium:	1 to 2 feet of growth per year
Fast:	More than 2 feet of growth per year.

Flowering Dogwood

Honey Locust

HEIGHT Tall

Mockernut Hickory

Diameter

A third dimensional characteristic of trees often considered by landscape architects and foresters is their diameter (generally measured at a height of 4½ feet). For example, trees with potentially large, rapidly increasing diameter when planted adjacent to sidewalks or other permanent structures often create extreme stresses from their size and rooting habits, causing damage such as cracking and buckling of the permanent surface.

The following diameter classes were developed for trees growing under normal forest competition from woody vegetation. (Therefore, an open-grown tree can be expected to increase in diameter at a faster rate.)

DIAMETER AT MATURITY:
Small: less than 1 foot
Medium: 1 to 2 feet
Large: 2 to 3 feet
Very Large: 3 feet or more

GROWTH RATE:
Slow: less than ¼ inch per year
Medium: ¼ to ½ inch per year
Fast: ½ inch per year or more

Hawthorn

Shagbark Hickory

Swamp White Oak

2. Height and diameter at maturity and growth rate.

Tree species	Total height	Total diameter	GROWTH RATE Height	Diameter
Ash, Green	medium; tall	medium to large	medium	medium
Ash, White	tall	large	medium	medium
Basswood, American	tall; very tall	large to very large	slow	slow
Beech, American	tall; very tall	large to very large	slow	slow
Birch, River	tall	large	medium	medium
Buckeye, Ohio	medium	medium	slow	slow
Catalpa	tall	medium to large	medium	medium
Cedar, Eastern Red	medium	medium	slow	slow
Cherry, Black	medium; tall	medium to large	medium	medium
Cottonwood, Eastern	very tall	large to very large	fast	fast
Crab Apple	very small	small	medium	slow
Cucumber Tree	medium; tall	medium to large	medium	medium
Dogwood, Flowering	very small	small	medium	slow
Elm, American	tall; very tall	large to very large	medium	medium
Elm, Slippery	tall; very tall	large	medium	medium
Gum, Black	very tall	very large	medium	medium
Gum, Sweet	tall; very tall	large to very large	medium	medium
Hackberry	medium; tall	medium to large	slow	slow
Hawthorn	very small	small	slow	slow
Hickory, Bitternut	tall	medium to large	medium	slow
Hickory, Mockernut	tall	large	slow	slow
Hickory, Pignut	tall	large	slow	slow
Hickory, Shagbark	tall; very tall	medium to large	slow	slow
Hickory, Shellbark	very tall	very large	slow	slow
Hornbeam, American	very small; small	small	slow	slow
Hornbeam, Hop	very small; small	small	slow	slow
Locust, Black	medium	medium to large	medium; fast	medium
Locust, Honey	medium; tall; very tall	large	medium	slow
Maple, Black	tall; very tall	large	medium	medium
Maple, Red	medium; tall	medium to large	medium	medium
Maple, Silver	tall; very tall	large to very large	medium	medium
Maple, Sugar	tall; very tall	large	medium	medium

SIZE

Table 2. (*continued*)

| Tree species | Total height | Total diameter | GROWTH RATE | |
			Height	Diameter
Oak, Black	tall; very tall	large	medium	medium
Oak, Bur	tall; very tall	medium to very large	slow	medium
Oak, Chinkapin	tall	large	slow	medium
Oak, Northern Red	very tall	large	medium	medium
Oak, Pin	tall	large	medium	medium
Oak, Post	medium	medium	slow	slow
Oak, Shingle	medium	large	medium	medium
Oak, Swamp White	tall; very tall	large	slow	slow
Oak, White	very tall	very large	slow	medium
Osage Orange	small	small to medium	medium	medium
Persimmon	small; medium	medium	slow	slow
Pine, Eastern White	very tall	large	medium; fast	medium
Poplar, Tulip	very tall	large to very large	fast	medium; fast
Redbud, Eastern	very small	small	slow	slow
Sassafras	small; medium	medium	fast	medium
Sycamore	tall; very tall	very large	medium; fast	medium
Walnut, Black	tall; very tall	large to very large	fast	medium
Willow, Black	very tall	medium	fast	slow

Shape of leaf

The shape of tree leaves, when present in a variety, develop interest and curiosity in the viewer. They also are valuable for identification purposes. Leaves, unlike flowers or fruits, are present during the major summer outdoor recreation season.

The following classification of leaf shape is generally accepted.

Figure 2

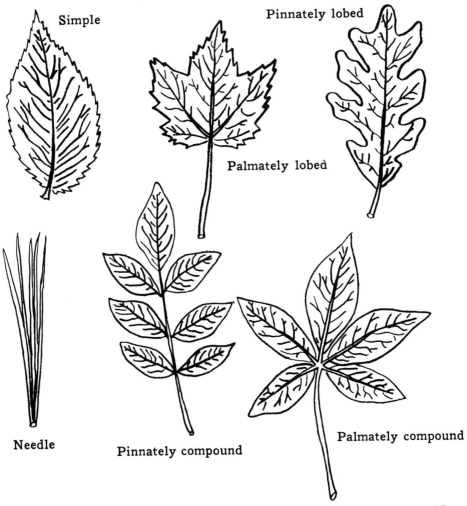

Simple

Pinnately lobed

Palmately lobed

Needle

Pinnately compound

Palmately compound

American Basswood

American Beech

River Birch

Catalpa

Black Cherry

Eastern Cottonwood

Crab Apple

Cucumber Tree

Flowering Dogwood

American Elm

Slippery Elm

Black Gum

Hackberry

Hawthorn

American Hornbeam

Hop Hornbeam

Shingle Oak

Osage Orange

Persimmon

Eastern Redbud

Black Willow

Sweet Gum

Black Maple

Red Maple

Silver Maple

Sugar Maple

Tulip Poplar

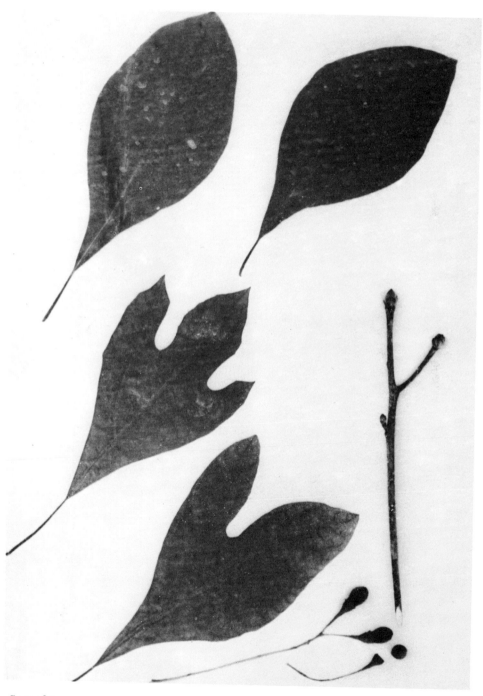

Sassafras

Sycamore

Black Oak

Bur Oak

66

Chinkapin Oak

LEAVES   Pinnately lobed

Northern Red Oak

Pin Oak

Post Oak

Swamp White Oak

White Oak

Ohio Buckeye

Green Ash

White Ash

Bitternut Hickory

Mockernut Hickory

Pignut Hickory

Shagbark Hickory

Shellbark Hickory

Black Locust

Honey Locust

Black Walnut

Eastern Red Cedar.

Eastern White Pine

LEAVES

Color of fall foliage

During the autumn season, many of the trees in the Central and Eastern hardwoods region display a brilliant coloration of foliage. This colorful display attracts people into the countryside.

Through manipulation of vegetation, managers can enhance this beauty by encouraging species which have a desirable fall color. The predominant foliage color of the majority of trees is yellow, but it is the other contrasting colors which make autumn color of outstanding beauty.

Six colors represent the majority of hues of the leaves in the fall:

Red to Scarlet
Yellow
Purple
Brown
Orange
Green (Evergreen)

3. Shape and fall color of leaves.

Tree species	Shape	Fall color range
Ash, Green	pinnately compound	yellow
Ash, White	pinnately compound	yellow; purple
Basswood, American	simple	yellow
Beech, American	simple	yellow
Birch, River	simple	yellow
Buckeye, Ohio	palmately compound	orange
Catalpa	simple	yellow; brown
Cedar, Eastern Red	needle	purple; brown; green
Cherry, Black	simple	red – scarlet
Cottonwood, Eastern	simple	yellow
Crab Apple	simple	brown
Cucumber Tree	simple	yellow
Dogwood, Flowering	simple	red – scarlet
Elm, American	simple	yellow
Elm, Slippery	simple	brown
Gum, Black	simple	red – scarlet
Gum, Sweet	palmately lobed	red; purple
Hackberry	simple	yellow
Hawthorn	simple, palmately lobed	red – scarlet; orange
Hickory, Bitternut	pinnately compound	yellow
Hickory, Mockernut	pinnately compound	yellow
Hickory, Pignut	pinnately compound	yellow
Hickory, Shagbark	pinnately compound	yellow
Hickory, Shellbark	pinnately compound	yellow
Hornbeam, American	simple	red; orange
Hornbeam, Hop	simple	yellow
Locust, Black	pinnately compound	yellow
Locust, Honey	pinnately compound	yellow
Maple, Black	palmately lobed	yellow
Maple, Red	palmately lobed	red – scarlet
Maple, Silver	palmately lobed	yellow
Maple, Sugar	palmately lobed	red; yellow; orange
Oak, Black	pinnately lobed	red – scarlet
Oak, Bur	pinnately lobed	brown
Oak, Chinkapin	pinnately lobed	red – scarlet

Table 3. (*continued*)

Tree species	Shape	Fall color range
Oak, Northern Red	pinnately lobed	red – scarlet
Oak, Pin	pinnately lobed	red – scarlet
Oak, Post	pinnately lobed	red – scarlet
Oak, Shingle	simple	red; yellow; brown
Oak, White Swamp	pinnately lobed	red – scarlet
Oak, White	pinnately lobed	red; purple
Osage Orange	simple	yellow
Persimmon	simple	red – scarlet
Pine, Eastern White	needle	green
Poplar, Tulip	palmately lobed	yellow
Redbud, Eastern	simple	yellow
Sassafras	simple, palmately lobed	red; yellow; orange
Sycamore	palmately lobed	yellow; brown
Walnut, Black	pinnately compound	yellow
Willow, Black	simple	brown

Bark

Texture

The bark of a tree should be considered as more than simply a protective cover. The tree's bark has beauty, design, and in many cases each tree has its own characteristic shape, form, and color. The surface that we see on the trunk and branches is dead, yet is far from being static. Rough bark will crack and split as the tree increases in size. Many of the species, such as oaks, elms, ashes, maples, and hickories, shed their characteristically shaped fragments due to the weathering process. The smooth-bark species, such as beech, are capable of great distension as the tree grows. These bark surfaces weather away without noticeable signs, but other species, such as the birches, visibly peel off in thin layers.

These distinctive textural characteristics of the bark are very useful for the purpose of identification and for adding variation in a developed area, especially during the leafless season.

Seven categories of bark texture are recognized:

Smooth
Peeling
Scaley
Deed-furrowed
Shallow-furrowed
Knobby
Blocky

American Beech

American Hornbeam

Shagbark Hickory

Silver Maple

Black Cherry

Honey Locust

Eastern Cottonwood

Bur Oak

Mockernut Hickory

Northern Red Oak

Hackberry

100

BARK   Blocky

Persimmon

Flowering Dogwood

Unique Twig Bark Formation: Sweet Gum

Color

Bark color, like bark texture, is a distinctive characteristic of a tree which should not go unrecognized. Many trees can be readily identified at any season of the year by bark characteristics alone. Similar to the use of species with colorful fall foliage, proper placement of trees with various bark colors may establish harmony and/or contrast throughout the landscape.

If trees are placed properly, bark color may also serve as a tool. For example, on secondary roads with frequent sharp curves, trees with light-colored bark establish a contrasting background and reflect light at considerable distances to warn motorists of an oncoming curve.

In this category, five colors are recognized:

> **Gray to dark gray**
> **Black**
> **Dark brown**
> **Light brown**
> **Reddish brown**

Black Oak

American Elm

Thickness

When used in the park landscape, a tree may be subjected to many abuses that require bark protection. For example, people carve, chop, and through carelessness or lack of coordination, bump trees with their cars and trailers. Then too, trees near charcoal grills and campfires are subjected to considerable heat from fires.

Thin-barked trees do not have the insulation and, thus, the protection to the cambium layer as do the thicker-barked trees. The cambium layer is located directly inside the bark and is the area in which all growth in diameter takes place. If this area is damaged, it causes a loss in vigor and allows the easy entry of insects and disease, possibly followed by death.

A tree's bark thickness varies with its age and rate of growth. Older, slower-growing trees have thicker barks than younger, faster-growing ones.

Two degrees of bark thickness at a tree's maturity are recognized:

Thin bark: Less than three-fourths of an inch thick.
Thick bark: Greater than three-fourths of an inch thick.

BARK   Thick

Sugar Maple

Swamp White Oak

Hop Hornbeam

Sycamore

An Example of Carvings on a Thin-barked Tree

4. Bark texture, color, and thickness of mature trees

Tree species	Texture	Color range	Thickness
Ash, Green	shallow-furrowed	gray – dark gray	thick
Ash, White	shallow-furrowed	gray – dark gray	thick
Basswood, American	scaly; shallow-furrowed	gray; light brown	thin
Beech, American	smooth	gray – dark gray	thin
Birch, River	peeling	reddish brown	thin
Buckeye, Ohio	scaly	gray; light brown	thin
Catalpa	shallow-furrowed	reddish brown	thin
Cedar, Eastern Red	scaly; shallow-furrowed	reddish brown	thin
Cherry, Black	scaly; shallow-furrowed	black; reddish brown	thin
Cottonwood, Eastern	deep-furrowed	dark brown	thick
Crab Apple	scaly	reddish brown	thin
Cucumber Tree	scaly; shallow-furrowed	dark brown	thin
Dogwood, Flowering	blocky	black; reddish brown	thick
Elm, American	deep-furrowed; shallow-furrowed	gray – dark gray	thick
Elm, Slippery	deep-furrowed; shallowed-furrowed	reddish brown	thin
Gum, Black	blocky	gray; light brown	thin
Gum, Sweet	deep-furrowed	gray; dark – light brown	thick; thin
Hackberry	knobby	gray – dark gray	thin
Hawthorn	scaly	gray; reddish brown	thin
Hickory, Bitternut	smooth; shallow-furrowed	gray; light brown	thin
Hickory, Mockernut	shallow-furrowed	gray – dark gray	thin
Hickory, Pignut	shallow-furrowed	gray – dark gray	thin
Hickory, Shagbark	peeling	gray – dark gray	thin
Hickory, Shellbark	peeling	gray – dark gray	thick; thin
Hornbeam, American	smooth	gray; light brown	thin
Hornbeam, Hop	scaly; shallow-furrowed	gray; dark brown; light brown	thin
Locust, Black	deep-furrowed	black; reddish brown	thick
Locust, Honey	scaly; shallow-furrowed	gray; reddish brown	thin
Maple, Black	deep-furrowed	black	thick
Maple, Red	scaly; shallow-furrowed	gray – dark gray	thick

BARK

Table 4. (*continued*)

Tree species	Texture	Color range	Thickness
Maple, Silver	smooth; peeling	gray - dark gray; reddish brown	thick
Maple, Sugar	deep-furrowed; shallow-furrowed	gray	thick
Oak, Black	deep-furrowed	black	thick
Oak, Bur	deep-furrowed	gray–dark gray	thick
Oak, Chinkapin	scaly; deep-furrowed	gray–dark gray	thin
Oak, Nórthern Red	deep-furrowed; shallow-furrowed	dark brown	thick; thin
Oak, Pin	smooth; shallow-furrowed	gray; light brown	thick; thin
Oak, Post	deep-furrowed	reddish brown	thick
Oak, Shingle	shallow-furrowed	gray–dark gray	thick
Oak, Swamp White	deep-furrowed	dark brown	thick
Oak, White	shallow-furrowed; blocky	gray–dark gray	thick; thin
Osage Orange	shallow-furrowed	reddish brown	thin
Persimmon	blocky	black	thick
Pine, Eastern White	scaly; deep-furrowed; blocky	gray–dark gray	thick
Poplar, Tulip	deep-furrowed; shallow-furrowed	gray; light brown	thick; thin
Redbud, Eastern	scaly	black; dark brown; reddish brown	thin
Sassafras	deep-furrowed	reddish brown	thick; thin
Sycamore	smooth; peeling	yellow green	thin
Walnut, Black	deep-furrowed	dark brown; reddish brown	thick
Willow, Black	scaly; deep-furrowed; shallow-furrowed	black; dark brown	thick; thin

Flowers

Season

Flowers on trees, generally appearing in the beginning of the growing season, can add considerable color and beauty to the landscape. For example, eastern redbuds and flowering dogwoods are well known for tempering the starkness of the forest in early spring. In other areas, such as picnic and camp areas, along trails, and at scenic vistas or overlooks, flowering trees have often been planted to provide an en masse arrangement of blossoms.

Color

All but two trees, catalpa and American basswood, generally are finished flowering by June. However, many of the trees' flowers are so small that they are inconspicuous.

Five flower color classes are:

White to creamy white	Yellow to yellow-green
Purple to lavendar	Rust to brown
Pink to red	

Flowering habit

It should be pointed out that most trees have both male and female sex organs on the same flowers, or on different flowers of the same tree, allowing self-fertilization. Trees without this characteristic must be located near another tree of the opposite sex in order to be fertilized. Where seeding may be a nuisance, selection of a male tree would be desirable. The following trees are dioescious (of one sex):

Always dioecious:

Black Willow	Eastern Cottonwood	Persimmon

Sometimes dioecious:

Green Ash	Eastern Red Cedar	Silver Maple
White Ash	Black Locust	Sugar Maple
Black Gum	Honey Locust	Osage Orange
Eastern Redbud	Black Maple	Tulip Popular
	Red Maple	

A Flowering Dogwood in the Spring

Black Locust

Black Cherry

Crab Apple

Flowering Dogwood

Eastern Redbud

Green Ash

Sassafras

FLOWERS   Pink to red

Eastern Cottonwood

American Hornbeam

Cucumber Tree

Tulip Poplar

Sweet Gum

Black Maple

Ohio Buckeye

Red Maple

Hop Hornbeam

Northern Red Oak

5. *Flower color and visibility*

Tree species	Color range	Visibility
Ash, Green	purple – lavender; yellow – yellow-green	inconspicuous
Ash, White	purple – lavender	inconspicuous
Basswood, American	white; yellow – yellow-green	conspicuous
Beech, American	yellow – yellow-green	conspicuous
Birch, River	yellow – yellow-green	inconspicuous
Buckeye, Ohio	yellow – yellow-green	conspicuous
Catalpa	white	conspicuous
Cedar, Eastern Red	purple – lavender	inconspicuous
Cherry, Black	white	conspicuous
Cottonwood, Eastern	pink – red; yellow – yellow-green	inconspicuous
Crab Apple	white: pink – red	conspicuous
Cucumber Tree	yellow – yellow-green	conspicuous
Dogwood, Flowering	white	conspicuous
Elm, American	pink – red; yellow – yellow-green	inconspicuous
Elm, Slippery	purple – lavender	inconspicuous
Gum, Black	white	inconspicuous
Gum, Sweet	yellow – yellow-green	conspicuous
Hackberry	white; yellow – yellow-green	inconspicuous
Hawthorn	white; pink – red	conspicuous
Hickory, Bitternut	yellow – yellow-green	inconspicuous
Hickory, Mockernut	yellow – yellow-green	inconspicuous
Hickory, Pignut	yellow – yellow-green	inconspicuous
Hickory, Shagbark	yellow – yellow-green	inconspicuous
Hickory, Shellbark	yellow – yellow-green	inconspicuous
Hornbeam, American	pink – red; yellow – yellow-green	inconspicuous
Hornbeam, Hop	rust – brown	inconspicuous
Locust, Black	white	conspicuous
Locust, Honey	yellow – yellow-green	conspicuous
Maple, Black	yellow – yellow-green	conspicuous
Maple, Red	pink – red; rust – brown	conspicuous
Maple, Silver	pink – red; yellow –yellow-green	inconspicuous
Maple, Sugar	yellow – yellow-green	inconspicuous
Oak, Black	yellow – yellow-green	inconspicuous
Oak, Bur	yellow – yellow-green	inconspicuous
Oak, Chinkapin	yellow – yellow-green	inconspicuous

Table 5. (*continued*)

Tree species	Color range	Visibility
Oak, Northern Red	rust – brown	inconspicuous
Oak, Pin	pink – red	inconspicuous
Oak, Post	yellow – yellow-green	inconspicuous
Oak, Shingle	yellow – yellow-green	inconspicuous
Oak, Swamp White	yellow – yellow-green	inconspicuous
Oak, White	yellow – yellow-green	inconspicuous
Osage Orange	yellow – yellow-green	inconspicuous
Persimmon	white; yellow – yellow-green	conspicuous
Pine, Eastern White	purple – lavender; pink – red; yellow-green	inconspicuous
Poplar, Tulip	yellow – yellow-green	conspicuous
Redbud, Eastern	purple – lavender	conspicuous
Sassafras	purple – lavender	inconspicuous
Sycamore	pink – red; yellow – yellow-green	inconspicuous
Walnut, Black	yellow – yellow-green	conspicuous
Willow, Black	yellow – yellow-green	inconspicuous

Type

There are three basic types of fruit produced by trees:

Fleshy fruit: fruits that have soft external coverings over the seed.

Nut or seed: fruits that have hard or leathery external coverings over the seed, or exist in seed form.

Cone: The woody, scaly fruit of evergreen trees, having stiff scales which carry the seed.

The type of fruit is of major concern where the fruit may have desirable or undesirable characteristics. For example, certain fleshy fruits when crushed give off an odor and stain clothing; among these are osage orange, persimmon, crab apple, and catalpa.

Black Gum

Cucumber Tree

Sycamore

American Basswood

Tulip Poplar

American Elm

Swamp White Oak

Sweet Gum

Ohio Buckeye

Sugar Maple

Eastern Cottonwood

FRUIT   Seed

Green Ash

Slippery Elm

Eastern White Pine

Color

Two desirable characteristics of the fruits are their color and whether or not they are edible. Just as most trees flower in the spring, most have fruit in the fall. Fruit colors often lend beauty to the landscape in the same way as flowers.

Seven fruit colors are:

Black
Blue to purple
Red to scarlet
Yellow to brown
Orange
Green
White to gray

Edibility

The fruits edible by wildlife are separated into two major divisions and rated as a food which is highly desirable or as a food which is taken only in the case of an emergency due to food shortage.

Two general categories of fruit edibility were formed: wildlife consumption—birds and animals—and human consumption.

Trees are a major source of food for many wildlife species. The acorns produced by the oaks are considered to be the food most consumed by the largest variety of wildlife species. Birds eat the fruit or seed of all the species considered in this study except bitternut hickory, pignut hickory, Ohio buckeye, and black locust. The fruit of the bitternut hickory is too bitter to be edible, and it has been noted that even the squirrels usually ignore it. Even though birds consume fruit from all but four of the trees, many of these fruits are only taken as emergency foods.

Animals, from field mice to white-tailed deer, at one time or another, consume fruit or seed from all the fifty trees except black locust, cottonwood, and sycamore, yet only twenty-two are considered highly desirable, the oaks making up almost one-half of this category. The cottonwood and sycamore have very small seeds and are probably not eaten by animals for that reason. The black locust seed has a tough, hard outer covering which makes it almost impossible to be digested by animals; and if it is ingested, it soon passes out in the feces products. The honey locust seed is similar to that of the black locust.

Fruits and seeds of ten trees have been used for human consumption. These are: shagbark and shellbark hickory, mockernut hickory, hawthorn, crab apple, persimmon, American beech, black walnut, black cherry, and white oak. It is important to note that the Ohio buckeye's fruit is considered poisonous to humans. Care should be taken not to eat persimmon fruit until after it has fallen to the ground or after the first hard frost. If eaten after being picked from the tree, the fruit is very puckery.

White **Oak**

Black Cherry

Crab Apple

American Beech

Black Walnut

Persimmon

Hawthorn

Mockernut Hickory

Shagbark Hickory

Shellbark Hickory

Osage Orange

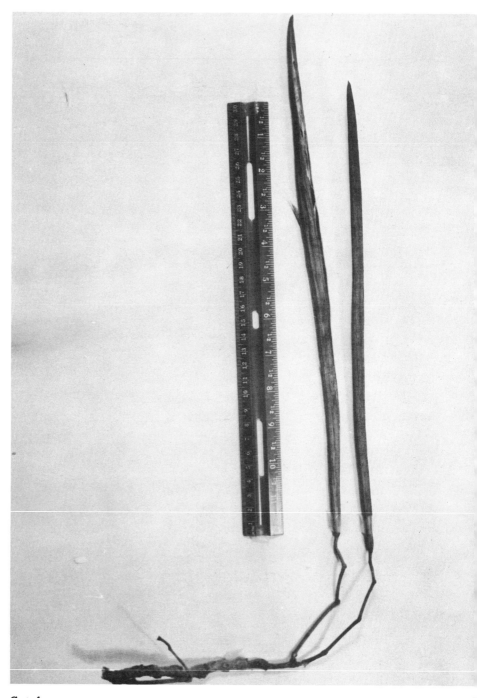

Catalpa

Crab Apple

Persimmon

6. Type, color, and edibility of tree fruits

Tree species	Type	Color range	Edibility	Wildlife rating
Ash, Green	nut or seed	yellow – brown; green	birds; animals	low
Ash, White	nut or seed	yellow – brown; green	birds; animals	low
Basswood, American	nut or seed	yellow – brown; white – gray	birds; animals	low
Beech, American	nut or seed	yellow – brown	humans; birds; animals	high
Birch, River	nut or seed	yellow – brown	birds; animals	low
Buckeye, Ohio	nut or seed	yellow – brown	animals	low
Catalpa	nut or seed	yellow – brown	birds; animals	low
Cedar, Eastern Red	fleshy	blue – purple	birds; animals	high
Cherry, Black	fleshy	black; red – scarlet	human; birds; animals	high
Cottonwood, Eastern	nut or seed	yellow – brown; white – gray; green	birds	low
Crab Apple	fleshy	red – scarlet; green	humans; birds; animals	high
Cucumber Tree	fleshy	red – scarlet	birds; animals	low
Dogwood, Flowering	fleshy	red – scarlet	birds; animals	high
Elm, American	fleshy	yellow – brown	birds; animals	low
Elm, Slippery	nut or seed	yellow – brown	birds; animals	low
Gum, Black	fleshy	blue – purple	birds; animals	high
Gum, Sweet	nut or seed	yellow – brown	birds; animals	low
Hackberry	fleshy	blue – purple	birds; animals	low
Hawthorn	fleshy	red – scarlet; green	humans; birds; animals	high
Hickory, Bitternut	nut or seed	yellow – brown; green	animals	medium
Hickory, Mockernut	nut or seed	yellow – brown; green	humans; birds; animals	high
Hickory, Pignut	nut or seed	yellow – brown; green	animals	medium
Hickory, Shagbark	nut or seed	green	humans; birds; animals	high
Hickory, Shellbark	nut or seed	yellow – brown; orange; green	humans; birds; animals	high
Hornbeam, American	nut or seed	yellow – brown	birds; animals	low
Hornbeam, Hop	nut or seed	yellow – brown	birds; animals	low
Locust, Black	nut or seed	yellow – brown	. . .	low
Locust, Honey	nut or seed	yellow – brown	birds; animals	low

FRUIT

Table 6. (*continued*)

Tree species	Type	Color range	Edibility	Wildlife rating
Maple, Black	fleshy; nut or seed	yellow – brown	birds; animals	medium
Maple, Red	fleshy; nut or seed	yellow – brown	birds; animals	low
Maple, Silver	fleshy; nut	yellow – brown	birds; animals	low
Maple, Sugar	fleshy; nut or seed	yellow – brown	birds; animals	medium
Oak, Black	nut or seed	yellow – brown; green	birds; animals	high
Oak, Bur	nut or seed	yellow – brown; green	birds; animals	high
Oak, Chinkapin	nut or seed	yellow – brown; green	birds; animals	high
Oak, Northern Red	nut or seed	yellow – brown; green	birds, animals	high
Oak, Pin	nut or seed	Yellow – brown; green	birds, animals	high
Oak, Post	nut or seed	yellow – brown; green	birds; animals	high
Oak, Shingle	nut or seed	yellow – brown; green	birds; animals	high
Oak, Swamp White	nut or seed	yellow – brown; green	birds; animals	high
Oak, White	nut or seed	yellow – brown; green	humans; birds; animals	high
Osage Orange	fleshy	yellow – brown; green	birds; animals	medium
Persimmon	fleshy	orange	humans; birds; animals	high
Pine, Eastern White	cone	yellow – brown	birds; animals	low
Poplar, Tulip	nut or seed	yellow – brown	birds; animals	low
Redbud, Eastern	nut or seed	red – scarlet	birds; animals	low
Sassafras	fleshy	black; blue – purple	birds; animals	high
Sycamore	nut or seed	yellow – brown	birds	low
Walnut, Black	fleshy; nut or seed	green	humans; birds; animals	high
Willow, Black	nut or seed	yellow – brown	birds; animals	low

Longevity

Of prime importance when selecting a tree to plant is how long it will live. Three age-classifications follow:

Short-lived:	60 years or less
Medium-lived:	60 to 150 years
Long-lived:	150 years or more

These classifications may be useful not only for estimating the longevity of a seedling, but for determining the length of time remaining for existing established trees. To insure a continuous forest canopy, under-planting and interplanting should begin several years before older trees become decadent and hazardous.

Crab Apple

Sugar Maple

White Oak

7. Longevity

Tree species	Longevity
Ash, Green	medium-lived
Ash, White	long-lived
Basswood, American	medium-lived
Beech, American	long-lived
Birch, River	medium-lived
Buckeye, Ohio	medium-lived
Catalpa	medium-lived
Cedar, Eastern Red	long-lived
Cherry, Black	medium-lived
Cottonwood, Eastern	short-lived
Crab Apple	short-lived
Cucumber Tree	medium-lived
Dogwood, Flowering	short-lived
Elm, American	long-lived
Elm, Slippery	medium-lived
Gum, Black	medium-lived
Gum, Sweet	long-lived
Hackberry	long-lived
Hawthorn	short-lived
Hickory, Bitternut	long-lived
Hickory, Mockernut	long-lived
Hickory, Pignut	long-lived
Hickory, Shagbark	long-lived
Hickory, Shellbark	long-lived
Hornbeam, American	short-lived
Hornbeam, Hop	short-lived
Locust, Black	short-lived
Locust, Honey	medium-lived
Maple, Black	medium-lived
Maple, Red	medium-lived
Maple, Silver	medium-lived
Maple, Sugar	medium-lived
Oak, Black	medium-lived
Oak, Bur	long-lived
Oak, Chinkapin	long-lived

Table 7. (*continued*)

Tree species	Longevity
Oak, Northern Red	long-lived
Oak, Pin	medium-lived
Oak, Post	medium-lived
Oak, Shingle	long-lived
Oak, Swamp White	long-lived
Oak, White	long-lived
Osage Orange	long-lived
Persimmon	short-lived
Pine, Eastern White	long-lived
Poplar, Tulip	long-lived
Redbud, Eastern	short-lived
Sassafras	medium-lived
Sycamore	long-lived
Walnut, Black	long-lived
Willow, Black	short-lived

Rooting pattern

Root pattern is a tree characteristic many times overlooked when establishing a tree for recreational use. It has been demonstrated that the amounts of recreational traffic a tree can withstand is influenced by its root system. Some species have a tendency to be shallow-rooted while others generally establish a strong, deep-penetrating root system. In general, the shallow, lateral-rooted trees are relatively fast growing, require an abundance of moisture in the upper soil layers and are subject to early injury during periods of low precipitation or low available soil moisture. As a result, they are very sensitive to soil compaction resulting from heavy foot or vehicular traffic. Therefore, shallow-rooted trees should be planted in areas where the ground water is high. Surfacing (blacktop or concrete), a popular recreation management technique, when applied in an area containing shallow-rooted trees may be detrimental if the surface eliminates water penetration in the upper soil layers and denies the tree its major moisture source.

Trees of the group having deep or intermediate root systems are not so soon affected by compaction, especially if deep soil moisture is available. Root penetration of the trees in this group is to a depth where moisture is available through the ground water source; thus, the trees are not so dependent on soil moisture in the upper soil layers.

Figure 3, which is a drawing of the root systems of native (not planted trees, is presented as an illustration. This figure serves to illustrate that many root systems are adaptable to the site conditions. Yet, for best growth and production a tree should be on a site where it can take advantage of its inherent system of rooting. Light watering of a young planted tree will also cause the shallow type of root system illustrated in *Figure 3*. When a tree is watered and only enough water is applied to wet the surface, a shallow root system develops and becomes dependent upon this surface water. Then, during a period of drought the tree has no deep-penetrating roots to the deep soil moisture supply. Therefore, if watering is used to aid in establishment of planted stock, the soil should be saturated to a good depth around each tree..

The trees are categorized into those with or without a deep taproot system of rooting:

Taproot System: Trees whose major root system has a main root which strikes downward with or without heavy branching until it either reaches an impenetrable layer or one so lacking in oxygen and/or moisture that further downward growth is impossible.

Diffuse (Lateral) System: Trees whose roots are made up of many branches which are closer to the soil surface than those trees whose main root system is a deep taproot.

3. Root Pattern Variations.

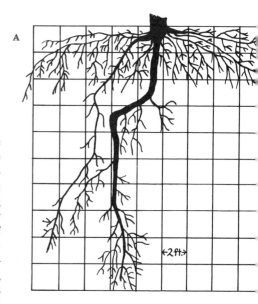

Root system (a) of 30-year-old native open-grown American elm in dune sand. Height of tree, 17 feet; diameter, at 4½ feet high, 6.3 inches; vigor, fair; care received during growth, none. Topography, strongly rolling; subsoil, fine sand; depth of water table, 20 feet. Root system (b) of 50-year-old native dominant American elm in clay loam. Height of tree, 45 feet; diameter, at 4½ feet, 11.8 inches; vigor fair; care received during growth, none. Topography, level; subsoil, silty clay loam; depth of water table, approximately 15 feet.

Shallow roots exposed on a forest trail

8. Rooting patterns

Tree species	Pattern
Ash, Green	diffuse
Ash, White	diffuse
Basswood, American	diffuse
Beech, American	diffuse
Birch, River	diffuse
Buckeye, Ohio	taproot
Catalpa	taproot
Cedar, Eastern Red	taproot
Cherry, Black	diffuse
Cottonwood, Eastern	diffuse
Crab Apple	diffuse
Cucumber Tree	diffuse
Dogwood, Flowering	diffuse
Elm, American	taproot; diffuse
Elm, Slippery	diffuse
Gum, Black	taproot
Gum, Sweet	taproot; diffuse
Hackberry	diffuse
Hawthorn	taproot
Hickory, Bitternut	taproot
Hickory, Mockernut	taproot
Hickory, Pignut	taproot
Hickory, Shagbark	taproot
Hickory, Shellbark	taproot
Hornbeam, American	diffuse
Hornbeam, Hop	diffuse
Locust, Black	diffuse
Locust, Honey	taproot; diffuse
Maple, Black	diffuse
Maple, Red	diffuse
Maple, Silver	diffuse
Maple, Sugar	diffuse
Oak, Black	taproot
Oak, Bur	taproot
Oak, Chinkapin	taproot

Table 8. (*continued*)

Tree species	Pattern
Oak, Northern Red	taproot
Oak, Pin	taproot: diffuse
Oak, Post	taproot
Oak, Shingle	taproot
Oak, Swamp White	diffuse
Oak, White	taproot
Osage Orange	diffuse
Persimmon	taproot
Pine, Eastern White	taproot
Poplar, Tulip	diffuse
Redbud, Eastern	diffuse
Sassafras	diffuse
Sycamore	diffuse
Walnut, Black	taproot
Willow, Black	diffuse

179

Natural pruning characteristics

In an area to be developed for camping, picnicking, or other uses where a tree's primary purpose is to provide shade, trees which are poor natural pruners should not be emphasized in planting. A tree which has a tendency to retain its limbs, and often has very little clear bole (trunk) will take up excess room, is hazardous, and the area beneath the tree cannot be properly utilized. Most species can be pruned, yet, when done properly, pruning is a costly operation which could be avoided if good natural pruning species are used. Then too, pruning many times opens the tree to disease and insect attack.

On the other hand, if trees are planted for screening purposes, species which are poor natural pruners are highly desirable. The persistent lower branches aid in producing a screen eliminating an undesirable view or absorbing noises from roads, buildings, machinery, animals, and people.

Caution should be exercised in the sudden opening of a stand of trees whose boles have been shaded for a long period of time. Sudden exposure to sunlight may cause sunscald or stimulate a great number of epicormic branches along the bole.

Three categories of limb retention are recognized:

Good pruning: A tree which does not retain large branches of its bole and is often clear-boled for one-half or more of its total height.

Fair pruning: A tree which has a tendency to retain some large branches usually on the lower part of the bole and is seldom clear-boled for more than one-half of its total height.

Poor pruning: A tree which has a tendency to retain its limbs, either dead or alive, and usually has very little clear bole.

A Poor Natural Pruning Tree: Pin Oak

A Tree with an Abundance of Epicormic Branches: Persimmon

A Tree Suitable for Screening: Eastern Red Cedar

9. Natural pruning characteristics (forest grown)

Tree species	Self-pruning capacity
Ash, Green	good
Ash, White	good
Basswood, American	good
Beech, American	fair; poor
Birch, River	fair
Buckeye, Ohio	good
Catalpa	poor
Cedar, Eastern Red	poor
Cherry, Black	good
Cottonwood, Eastern	good
Crab Apple	poor
Cucumber Tree	good
Dogwood, Flowering	poor
Elm, American	good
Elm, Slippery	good; fair
Gum, Black	good
Gum, Sweet	good
Hackberry	fair
Hawthorn	poor
Hickory, Bitternut	good
Hickory, Mockernut	good
Hickory, Pignut	good
Hickory, Shagbark	good
Hickory, Shellbark	good
Hornbeam, American	poor
Hornbeam, Hop	poor
Locust, Black	good
Locust, Honey	fair, poor
Maple, Black	fair
Maple, Red	fair
Maple, Silver	fair
Maple, Sugar	fair
Oak, Black	fair
Oak, Bur	fair
Oak, Chinkapin	fair

Table 9. (*continued*)

Tree species	Self-pruning capacity
Oak, Northern Red	good
Oak, Pin	poor
Oak, Post	poor
Oak, Shingle	poor
Oak, Swamp White	fair
Oak, White	good; fair
Osage Orange	poor
Persimmon	fair
Pine, Eastern White	poor
Poplar, Tulip	good
Redbud, Eastern	poor
Sassafras	good
Sycamore	good
Walnut, Black	good
Willow, Black	fair

Coppice potential

The coppice-potential classification deals primarily with the tree's ability to reproduce vegetatively, or simply the ability to "sprout." In the development of a park, a tree's ability to reproduce vegetatively could be an aid or a hindrance. The use of vegetative reproduction can be helpful in the rapid reforestation of a cleared area. As a general rule, vegetatively reproduced sprouts may be expected to attain larger size in a shorter period of time than trees grown from seeds. This rapid early growth of young sprouts is generally accounted for by the presence of an extensive root system established by the parent tree and the stored supply of carbohydrates in its root system.

However, with rapid growth in the younger stages comes more rapid deterioration in the older stages. It is generally considered that the life expectancy of a vegetatively reproduced tree is shorter; the form of the tree is often poor; and the incidence of rot is high. Therefore, if vegetative reproduction methods are used, it must be kept in mind that the tree's maximum age will not be reached and its maximum size will be smaller.

Time of cutting sprouting species is also an important factor to recognize. Cuttings made during the tree's dormant period (fall and winter) may lead to much more vigorous sprouting than those made during late spring and summer. Food reserves in the roots are at a maximum during the dormant period and at a minimum immediately after the formation of new leaves.

Sprouting often occurs almost immediately after cutting late in the growing season, but the young shoots barely have time to establish themselves before the first hard freeze. The young shoots are thus killed by frost and undesirable sprouting is checked.

Often young trees are damaged by campers and picknickers seeking long, green sticks to roast weiners or marshmallows. Should this be the problem, it might be feasible to cut small saplings of species which sprout and inform the people that these sprouts may be used. This may serve to deter them from damaging other trees whose prime purpose is for shade and beauty.

Three classes were formed in this category:

Non-sprouters: Trees that do not sprout when cut or wounded.

Sprouters: Trees that sprout from the stump and/or root collar when cut or wounded, but the number of sprouts is usually small.

Profuse sprouters: Trees that send up an abundance of sprouts from the stump and/or root collar when cut or wounded. Sprouts often form a thicket or clump because of the number of shoots.

A Sprouting Tree: Shellbark Hickory

A Profuse Sprouter: Willow

10. Coppice

Tree species	Coppice potential
Ash, Green	sprouter
Ash, White	profuse sprouter
Basswood, American	profuse sprouter
Beech, American	sprouter
Birch, River	sprouter
Buckeye, Ohio	sprouter
Catalpa	sprouter
Cedar, Eastern Red	non-sprouter
Cherry, Black	sprouter; profuse sprouter
Cottonwood, Eastern	sprouter
Crab Apple	sprouter
Cucumber Tree	profuse sprouter
Dogwood, Flowering	profuse sprouter
Elm, American	profuse sprouter
Elm, Slippery	profuse sprouter
Gum, Black	sprouter
Gum, Sweet	sprouter
Hackberry	sprouter
Hawthorn	sprouter
Hickory, Bitternut	profuse sprouter
Hickory, Mockernut	profuse sprouter
Hickory, Pignut	profuse sprouter
Hickory, Shagbark	profuse sprouter
Hickory, Shellbark	profuse sprouter
Hornbeam, American	sprouter
Hornbeam, Hop	non-sprouter
Locust, Black	sprouter
Locust, Honey	sprouter
Maple, Black	sprouter
Maple, Red	profuse sprouter
Maple, Silver	profuse sprouter
Maple, Sugar	sprouter
Oak, Black	profuse sprouter
Oak, Bur	sprouter
Oak, Chinkapin	sprouter

Table 10. (*continued*)

Tree species	Coppice potential
Oak, Northern Red	profuse sprouter
Oak, Pin	sprouter; profuse sprouter
Oak, Post	profuse sprouter
Oak, Shingle	sprouter
Oak, Swamp White	sprouter
Oak, White	sprouter; profuse sprouter
Osage Orange	sprouter
Persimmon	sprouter
Pine, Eastern White	non-sprouter
Poplar, Tulip	profuse sprouter
Redbud, Eastern	sprouter
Sassafras	profuse sprouter
Sycamore	sprouter; profuse sprouter
Walnut, Black	sprouter
Willow, Black	profuse sprouter

Succession stage

Knowledge of successional types of tree species may be desired by the recreational planner. This classification gives recognition of a species' natural position among plants as they are associated with the change that takes place in plant communities. Nature is constantly striving to produce, on a given area, the highest type of plant species which that particular site is capable of supporting. The characteristics of all stands are determined by the kind, frequency, and magnitude of disturbances that have affected the sites in the past. Climax communities are, in this sense, results of long series of small, light disturbances while pioneer stages are the product of a catastrophe. For instance, the abandonment of agriculture land would be a "catastrophe" in the ecological sense. Land which has been cultivated and planted for many years is now left on its own for plant production. The species which will first occupy the site are the pioneer species. If these species are to be maintained, then cultural practices may be needed to maintain the existing site conditions.

Three types of successional stages are generally recognized:

Pioneer: The first trees to invade open areas such as old agricultural fields; these trees begin site amelioration for those that will follow.

Sub-climax: Species which follow pioneers and occupy an area only for a limited time before they are replaced by another climax species.

Climax: Trees which can maintain themselves on an area indefinitely and cannot be displaced except by climatic change or destruction by external forces. They usually succeed pioneer and sub-climax species.

192

The Pioneer Stage on an Abandoned Oil Field

The Sub-climax Stage: White Oak

The Climax Stage: Mixed Hardwood Forest

11. Succession stages

Tree species	Succession stage
Ash, Green	pioneer; sub-climax
Ash, White	pioneer; sub-climax
Basswood, American	sub-climax
Beech, American	climax
Birch, River	sub-climax
Buckeye, Ohio	sub-climax
Catalpa	pioneer
Cedar, Eastern Red	pioneer; sub-climax
Cherry, Black	pioneer; sub-climax
Cottonwood, Eastern	pioneer
Crab Apple	pioneer
Cucumber Tree	sub-climax
Dogwood, Flowering	sub-climax; climax
Elm, American	pioneer; sub-climax; climax
Elm, Slippery	sub-climax; climax
Gum, Black	climax
Gum, Sweet	pioneer; sub-climax
Hackberry	pioneer; sub-climax; climax
Hawthorn	pioneer
Hickory, Bitternut	sub-climax; climax
Hickory, Mockernut	sub-climax; climax
Hickory, Pignut	sub-climax; climax
Hickory, Shagbark	sub-climax; climax
Hickory, Shellbark	sub-climax; climax
Hornbeam, American	sub-climax
Hornbeam, Hop	sub-climax; climax
Locust, Black	pioneer
Locust, Honey	pioneer; sub-climax
Maple, Black	climax
Maple, Red	pioneer; sub-climax
Maple, Silver	pioneer; sub-climax
Maple, Sugar	climax
Oak, Black	sub-climax; climax
Oak, Bur	pioneer; sub-climax; climax
Oak, Chinkapin	sub-climax

Table 11. (*continued*)

Tree species	Succession stage
Oak, Northern Red	sub-climax; climax
Oak, Pin	pioneer; sub-climax
Oak, Post	climax
Oak, Shingle	sub-climax; climax
Oak, Swamp White	sub-climax
Oak, White	sub-climax; climax
Osage Orange	sub-climax
Persimmon	pioneer; sub-climax
Pine, Eastern White	sub-climax
Poplar, Tulip	pioneer; sub-climax
Redbud, Eastern	sub-climax
Sassafras	pioneer
Sycamore	pioneer; sub-climax
Walnut, Black	pioneer; sub-climax
Willow, Black	pioneer

Shade tolerance

Selecting a tree that will be healthy while growing beneath other trees is often essential. For example, many parks are dominated by over-mature trees in poor health. If these parks are to retain their natural atmosphere, new trees must be planted to take the place of the old.

The amount of light a particular tree needs depends on its leaves' light-utilization potential. However, shade tolerance, like all general biological laws, is a relative factor. A tree may be tolerant if other environmental conditions for its survival are good.

Three classes of shade tolerance follow:

Tolerant: Trees that will grow and survive in dense shade.

Intermediate: Trees that will grow and survive in partial shade or in small openings where they will receive full sunlight for short periods during the day.

Intolerant: Trees that will not grow in shade and need full sunlight for survival and best growth.

In general, when planting shade-tolerant trees, do not use them in areas where full sunlight prevails. Examples of better locations include a small opening in a forest canopy, the north side of tall buildings, or an open area which is shaded for a major portion of the day.

Intolerant trees will not do well in shaded areas. Therefore, these species should be given preference in the open area.

A Shade-tolerant Tree: Flowering Dogwood

Interplanting to insure perpetuity of trees

12. Shade tolerance

Tree species	Shade tolerance
Ash, Green	intermediate
Ash, White	tolerant – intermediate
Basswood, American	tolerant
Beech, American	tolerant
Birch, River	intolerant
Buckeye, Ohio	intermediate
Catalpa	intermediate – intolerant
Cedar, Eastern Red	intermediate
Cherry, Black	intolerant
Cottonwood, Eastern	intolerant
Crab Apple	intolerant
Cucumber Tree	intermediate
Dogwood, Flowering	tolerant
Elm, American	intermediate
Elm, Slippery	tolerant – intermediate
Gum, Black	intermediate
Gum, Sweet	intermediate – intolerant
Hackberry	tolerant – intermediate
Hawthorn	intolerant
Hickory, Bitternut	intermediate – intolerant
Hickory, Mockernut	intermediate – intolerant
Hickory, Pignut	intermediate – intolerant
Hickory, Shagbark	intermediate
Hickory, Shellbark	tolerant
Hornbeam, American	tolerant
Hornbeam, Hop	tolerant
Locust, Black	intolerant
Locust, Honey	intolerant
Maple, Black	tolerant
Maple, Red	intermediate
Maple, Silver	intermediate – intolerant
Maple, Sugar	tolerant
Oak, Black	intermediate
Oak, Bur	intermediate
Oak, Chinkapin	tolerant

Table 12. (*continued*)

Tree species	Shade tolerance
Oak, Northern Red	intermediate
Oak, Pin	intolerant
Oak, Post	intolerant
Oak, Shingle	intermediate
Oak, Swamp White	intermediate
Oak, White	intermediate
Osage Orange	intolerant
Persimmon	tolerant
Pine, Eastern White	intermediate
Poplar, Tulip	intolerant
Redbud, Eastern	tolerant
Sassafras	intolerant
Sycamore	intermediate – intolerant
Walnut, Black	intolerant
Willow, Black	intolerant

Insect attack susceptibility

Insect attack, a costly and wasteful problem, could often be avoided if species were selected that are generally resistant. Understanding the potential of a tree's insect enemies begins with the realization that the insect enemy is a parasite and the tree is the host. Fortunately, only a few of these dependent organisms attack with a force which is fatal to the host. If the parasite is detrimental to its host, to the point of destruction, its food supply would be eliminated. The parasite that kills its hosts, and thus its food supply, is very poorly adapted to its environment. This is why introduced insects often cause much more damage than do native parasites. The well-adapted parasite may cause little damage and will thus go almost unnoticed.

Two classifications are recognized:

Few insect enemies (generally resistant to insect attack).

Several insect enemies (often detrimental to the tree's appearance or survival).

A fire scar which makes a tree susceptible to insect attack and disease

Disease susceptibility

Practically all tree species in any given area are subject to one or more diseases. Some diseases cause little noticeable damage to the trees. Others, through severe damage to leaves, bark, branches, or roots, cause deformity, stunting, and possibly the eventual death of the trees.

Therefore, the value of an area for recreational development may be greatly reduced or completely destroyed by the presence of diseased trees. The removal of trees damaged or killed by disease is in most cases very costly.

The fatality of the Dutch elm disease, which threatens to wipe out the elms, generally eliminates the possibility of using them in the parklike landscape.

The two general classifications of disease importance are based on the number of principal diseases attacking each species and the resistance of the tree to attack:

Few diseases (generally resistant to disease attack).

Several diseases (many times detrimental to the tree's appearance or survival).

A diseased area on a hickory tree

13. Insect and disease susceptibility

Tree species	Insect enemies	Disease enemies
Ash, Green	several	few
Ash, White	several	several
Basswood, American	few	few
Beech, American	several	several
Birch, River	few	few
Buckeye, Ohio	few	few
Catalpa	few	few
Cedar, Eastern Red	few	several
Cherry, Black	few	few
Cottonwood, Eastern	few	few
Crab Apple	several	several
Cucumber Tree	few	few
Dogwood, Flowering	several	few
Elm, American	several	several
Elm, Slippery	several	several
Gum, Black	few	few
Gum, Sweet	few	few
Hackberry	few	few
Hawthorn	few	few
Hickory, Bitternut	few	few
Hickory, Mockernut	few	few
Hickory, Pignut	several	several
Hickory, Shagbark	several	few
Hickory, Shellbark	few	few
Hornbeam, American	few	few
Hornbeam, Hop	few	few
Locust, Black	several	few
Locust, Honey	several	few
Maple, Black	several	several
Maple, Red	several	several
Maple, Silver	few	few
Maple, Sugar	several	several
Oak, Black	several	several
Oak, Bur	few	several
Oak, Chinkapin	several	few

Table 13. (*continued*)

Tree species	Insect enemies	Disease enemies
Oak, Northern Red	several	several
Oak, Pin	few	few
Oak, Post	several	several
Oak, Shingle	few	few
Oak, Swamp White	few	few
Oak, White	several	several
Osage Orange	few	few
Persimmon	few	several
Pine, Eastern White	few	several
Poplar, Tulip	few	few
Redbud, Eastern	few	few
Sassafras	several	few
Sycamore	few	few
Walnut, Black	few	few
Willow, Black	few	few

SITE REQUIREMENTS

Natural range

Trees are their healthiest when living within their natural range. Healthy trees grow faster, have more dense and colorful foliage, and are better able to withstand negative site conditions, such as soil compaction, bark injury, disease and insects attacks, than their counterparts living outside their botanical range.

The natural range of the following trees includes the entire three states of Illinois, Indiana, and Ohio:

Green ash	Hop hornbeam
White ash	Black maple
Eastern red cedar	Silver maple
Black cherry	Sugar maple
Eastern cottonwood	Black oak
Crab apple	Northern red oak
American elm	Shingle oak
Slippery elm	White oak
Hawthorn	Eastern redbud
Bitternut hickory	Black willow
Shagbark hickory	Black walnut
American hornbeam	

Maps depicting the ranges of the remaining trees are presented in the Appendix. These range maps should be used as general guides. It is suggested by the authors that a local nurseryman be consulted as to the adaptability of specific trees to the locality and site in question.

Topographic position

Slope position

A second major consideration regarding the suitability of a tree for a particular site, is where the site is located relative to the topography (slope). The broad slope positions recognized are (*Fig. 4*):

Bottomland   An area of land adjacent to and associated with streams, rivers, lakes, or other natural water basins. These lands extend up to the contour of land that is rarely, if ever, flooded.

Upland: Any area of land that has a higher elevation than the bottomland.

Cove: A sheltered recess or hollow on the side of a hill or slope—within the upland.

The above classification of slope position is indicative of naturally seeded trees within the forest canopy. However, bottomland species may be planted and will survive on upland sites, but generally the bottomland site conditions must, in some way, be approximated.

Alterations in slope position affect the amount and quantity of moisture available to the tree. For example, bottomland species are often shallow-rooted and are not capable of reaching low ground levels for moisture as are the more deep-rooted upland species. On the other hand, upland trees when planted on the bottomland sites may be affected adversely by excess water which in turn limits root aeration.

Examples of treatments that may in part overcome the above effects would be: artificially watering to simulate bottomland conditions; construction of draining systems for upland conditions.

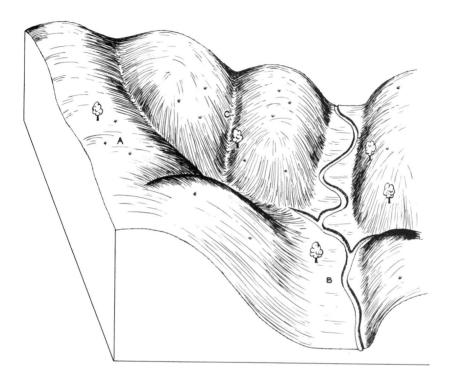

4. Drawing of Slope Positions:

(*a*) Upland, (*b*) Bottomland, (*c*) Cove. *From* Soils of Daviess County, Missouri," Missouri Agricultural Experiment Station Bulletin 604.

A Bottomland Site

214

An upland site

A cove site

Aspect (Direction of exposure)

The direction the slope faces is also important in areas of rapid change in topography, in that the aspect is directly related to surface temperature and thus the amount of moisture available for tree growth.

These categories of aspect are recognized:

North
South
Horizontal (bottomland, flat, no aspect).

Exposures to the south and southwest are subject to a concentration of direct sunrays and offer the presence of a prevailing wind during the warmer seasons. As a result, these sites generally have drier soil conditions and higher evapo-transpiration rates than other aspects.

Due to less sun exposure, the north and northeast slopes are cooler, more moist, and have lower soil temperatures. They also have deeper soils due to less rapid decomposition of humus matter. Therefore, trees selected for planting on north aspects, should be tolerant of lower soil temperatures and early frost.

It should be noted that upland trees, such as the oaks and hickories, that are rated as suitable for the southern aspect, may also be adaptable to some north-facing sites. However, these trees were rated according to where they occur naturally. For example, a major reason oaks are not found on northern aspects may be because of competition from faster growing, more mesophytic trees, and not the site conditions.

14. Topographic position

Tree species	Slope position	Aspect
Ash, Green	bottomland; upland	north; horizontal
Ash, White	cove; upland	north
Basswood, American	cove; upland	north
Beech, American	bottomland; cove	north
Birch, River	bottomland	horizontal
Buckeye, Ohio	bottomland	north
Catalpa	bottomland	north; south
Cedar, Eastern Red	upland	north; south
Cherry, Black	cove; upland	north
Cottonwood, Eastern	bottomland	horizontal
Crab Apple	upland	north
Cucumber Tree	bottomland; upland; cove	north
Dogwood, Flowering	bottomland; upland; cove	north; south
Elm, American	bottomland; upland; cove	north; south; horizontal
Elm, Slippery	bottomland; upland; cove	north
Gum, Black	bottomland; cove	north
Gum, Sweet	bottomland; upland; cove	north; south; horizontal
Hackberry	bottomland; upland	north
Hawthorn	bottomland; upland	north; south
Hickory, Bitternut	bottomland; upland	south; horizontal
Hickory, Mockernut	upland	south; horizontal
Hickory, Pignut	upland	north; south; horizontal
Hickory, Shagbark	cove; upland	south
Hickory, Shellbark	bottomland	south
Hornbeam, American	bottomland	north
Hornbeam, Hop	upland	north
Locust, Black	upland	north; south
Locust, Honey	bottomland; upland	north; south
Maple, Black	upland	north
Maple, Red	bottomland; upland	north; south
Maple, Silver	bottomland; cove	horizontal
Maple, Sugar	cove; upland	north; horizontal
Oak, Black	cove; upland	north; south
Oak, Bur	bottomland; upland	north; horizontal
Oak, Chinkapin	upland	north; south

Table 14. (*continued*)

Tree species	Slope position	Aspect
Oak, Northern Red	cove; upland	north
Oak, Pin	bottomland	horizontal
Oak, Post	upland	south
Oak, Shingle	bottomland; upland	south
Oak, Swamp White	bottomland	horizontal
Oak, White	cove; upland	north; south
Osage Orange	bottomland; upland	north; south
Persimmon	bottomland; upland; cove	north; south
Pine, Eastern White	cove; upland	north; south
Poplar, Tulip	cove; upland	north
Redbud, Eastern	bottomland; upland; cove	north; south
Sassafras	cove; upland	north; south
Sycamore	bottomland	horizontal
Walnut, Black	bottomland; upland; cove	north; south; horizontal
Willow, Black	bottomland	horizontal

Texture

The amount of water and oxygen readily available in the soil has an important effect on a tree's growth potential. A soil's texture generally determines the quality of aeration, amount of water movement, water availability, water-holding capacity, susceptibility to erosion, and degree of compaction.

Five major soil texture classes are generally recognized:

Coarse-texture soils
  Sands
  Loamy sands
Moderately coarse-textured soils
  Sandy loams
  Fine sandy loams
Medium-textured soils
  Very fine sandy loams
  Loams
  Silt loams
  Silts
Moderately fine-textured soils
  Clay loams
  Sandy clay loams
  Silty clay loams
Fine-textured soils
  Sandy clays
  Silty clays
  Clays

The following test can be used to roughly estimate the texture of soil. If a ball of moistened soil can easily be formed into a long, pliable ribbon, it is fine-textured. If a ribbon can be formed but breaks into pieces ¾ to 1 inch long, it is moderately fine-textured. If a ribbon cannot be formed and the soil feels very gritty, it is moderately coarse-textured. If the soil sample consists almost entirely of gritty material and leaves little or no stain on the hand, it is coarse-textured.

The fine-textured soils generally have the highest water-holding capacity, but the lowest aeration qualities. These soils often contain a high percentage of small clay particles which compact to form a hard layer on, or somewhat below, the soil surface. The amount of compaction depends upon the weight and frequency of the compacting agent. This impervious layer impedes the percolation of surface water, reduces aeration, and increases competition between plants for the reduced air and moisture. Generally, trees with lateral root systems are best able to adapt to these conditions.

On the other hand, coarse-textured soils contain large particles, such as sand. These soils usually have a rapid rate of water percolation and are well aerated. However, they have a low water-holding capacity and are therefore often dry. In addition, due to the rapid water movement, nutrient leaching is often a serious problem.

As a result, medium and moderately fine-textured soils, for most trees, provide the greatest growth potential. Fine-textured soils can be mechanically aerated and would benefit from the addition of sand particles, whereas coarse soils could be improved with an increase of organic matter.

Drainage

Six drainage classes are usually recognized:

Drainage Classes	Depth to Mottling*
Very poorly drained	0 inches, plus thick organic matter accumulation on surface plus permanently water-saturated soil
Poorly drained	0 to 6 inches
Somewhat poorly drained	6 to 16 inches
Moderately well-drained	16 to 30 inches
Well-drained	30 to 36 inches
Somewhat excessively drained	36 or more inches

Most trees attain their best development on moderate to well-drained sites. In addition to the factors discussed under soil texture, it is important to note that wet sites have cold soils which results in a much shorter growing season.

* Where the predominate soil color becomes irregularly marked with spots of different colors.

A Poorly Drained Bottomland Site

Soil reaction — pH

Chemically, the soil is divided into three classes based on reaction: acid, neutral, or alkaline. The degree of active acidity or alkalinity is measured by the use of a pH meter. Acid soils have a pH of 6.5 or less, alkaline ones have a pH above 7.5, and in neutral soils there is a balance of acid and alkaline materials, with a pH of 6.5 to 7.5.

When matching trees to soils, an effort to approximate the recommended pH requirements indicated in table 15 should be made. Doing this will help insure better survival and growth.

Lime may be used to increase the pH of a soil up to approximately 6.5 or near neutrality. To lower the pH, or increase the acidity, one of the following chemicals is often added to the soil: sulfur, aluminum sulfate, or calcium sulfate.

15. Soil conditions

Tree species	Texture	Drainage class	pH tolerance
Ash, Green	coarse to medium	somewhat poorly to well	very strongly acid to neu
Ash, White	coarse to medium	somewhat poorly to well	very strongly acid to neu
Basswood, American	moderately coarse; medium	moderately well; well	strongly acid to neutral
Beech, American	moderately coarse to moderately fine	moderately well; well	strongly acid; acid
Birch, River	coarse to fine	poorly to moderately well	very strongly acid to acid
Buckeye, Ohio	coarse to medium	somewhat poorly to well	acid
Catalpa	medium; moderately fine	moderately well; well	strongly acid to neutral
Cedar, Eastern Red	coarse to fine	somewhat poorly to somewhat excessively	strongly acid to alkaline
Cherry, Black	moderately coarse to moderately fine	moderately well; well	strongly acid to neutral
Cottonwood, Eastern	moderately coarse; medium	moderately well; well	very strongly acid to acid
Crab Apple	moderately coarse to fine	poorly to well	strongly acid to alkaline
Cucumber Tree	moderately coarse to moderately fine	moderately well; well	acid; neutral
Dogwood, Flowering	moderately coarse to moderately fine	moderately well; well	acid; neutral
Elm, American	coarse to moderately fine	very poorly to well	acid to alkalin
Elm, Slippery	moderately coarse to fine	moderately well; well	strongly acid to neutral
Gum, Black	coarse to moderately fine	moderately well; well	very strongly acid to neu
Gum, Sweet	moderately coarse to fine	poorly to moderately well	very strongly acid to neu
Hackberry	moderately coarse to moderately fine	somewhat poorly to well	neutral to alkaline
Hawthorn	moderately coarse to fine	somewhat poorly to somewhat excessively	strongly acid to neutral
Hickory, Bitternut	coarse to medium	somewhat poorly to well	strongly acid to alkaline
Hickory, Mockernut	coarse to fine	moderately well to somewhat excessively	strongly acid to neutral
Hickory, Pignut	medium to fine	moderately well; well	strongly acid; acid
Hickory, Shagbark	medium to fine	somewhat poorly to well to well	strongly acid to neutral
Hickory, Shellbark	coarse to medium	somewhat poorly to well	strongly acid to neutral
Hornbeam, American	medium to fine	poorly to somewhat excessively	very strongly acid to neu

e 15. (*continued*)

species	Texture	Drainage class	pH tolerance
beam, Hop	moderately coarse to fine	moderately well to somewhat excessively	strongly acid to alkaline
st, Black	moderately coarse to moderately fine	moderately well; well	very strongly acid to alkaline
st, Honey	moderately coarse to moderately fine	somewhat poorly to well	acid to alkaline
le, Black	coarse to medium	moderately well; well	neutral
e, Red	coarse to fine	very poorly to well	very strongly acid to neutral
le, Silver	moderately coarse to fine	poorly to well	acid; neutral
e, Sugar	coarse to medium	moderately well; well	strongly acid to neutral
Black	moderately coarse to moderately fine	moderately well; well	strongly acid to neutral
Bur	coarse to medium	somewhat poorly to well	strongly acid to neutral
Chinkapin	moderately coarse to moderately fine	well; somewhat excessively	neutral; alkaline
Northern Red	coarse to fine	moderately well; well	very strongly acid to neutral
Pin	moderately coarse to fine	poorly to well	very strongly acid to acid
Post	coarse to moderately fine	somewhat poorly to well	strongly acid to neutral
Shingle	coarse to medium	somewhat poorly to well	strongly acid to neutral
Swamp White	medium to fine	very poorly to somewhat poorly	very strongly acid to neutral
White	coarse to fine	moderately well to somewhat excessively	very strongly acid to neutral
e Orange	moderately coarse to moderately fine	somewhat poorly to somewhat excessively	strongly acid to alkaline
immon	medium; moderately fine	moderately well; well	acid
, Eastern White	coarse to fine	somewhat poorly to somewhat excessively	strongly acid to neutral
ar, Tulip	moderately coarse to moderately fine	moderately well; well	strongly acid to neutral
ud, Eastern	moderately coarse to moderately fine	moderately well; well	acid to alkaline
afras	moderately coarse; medium	well	very strongly acid to neutral
more	moderately coarse to moderately fine	poorly to well	very strongly acid to acid
nut, Black	moderately coarse to moderately fine	moderately well; well	acid; neutral
ow, Black	coarse to fine	very poorly to somewhat poorly	very strongly acid to neutral

225

APPENDIX/BIBLIOGRAPHY

Natural range for American Basswood

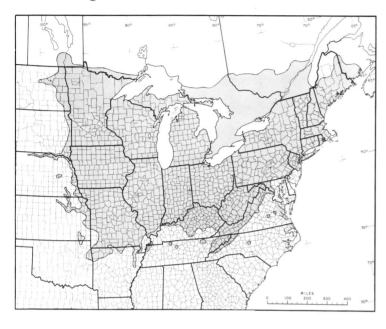

*Silvics of Forest
   Trees of the U.S.*
Agriculture Hand-
   book No. 271, 1965
U.S. Department of
   Agriculture
Forest Service,
   Washington, D.C.

Natural range for American Beech

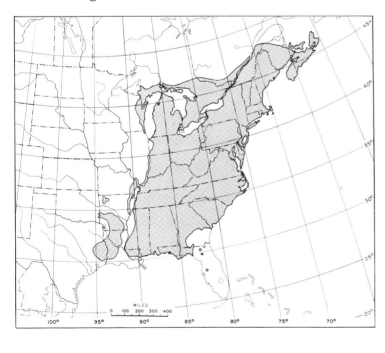

*Silvics of Forest
   Trees of the U.S.*
Agriculture Hand-
   book No. 271, 1965
U.S. Department of
   Agriculture
Forest Service,
   Washington, D.C.

229

Natural range for River Birch

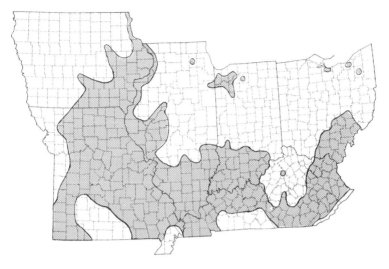

*Silvics of Forest
Trees of the U.S.*
Agriculture Hand-
book No. 271, 1965
U.S. Department of
Agriculture
Forest Service,
Washington, D.C.

Natural range for Ohio Buckeye

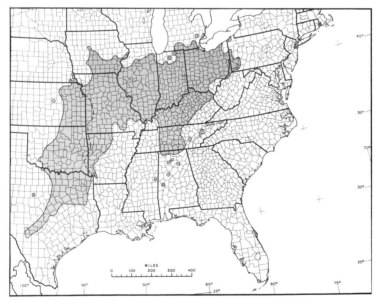

*Silvics of Forest
Trees of the U.S.*
Agriculture Hand-
book No. 271, 1965
U.S. Department of
Agriculture
Forest Service,
Washington, D.C.

Natural range for Catalpa

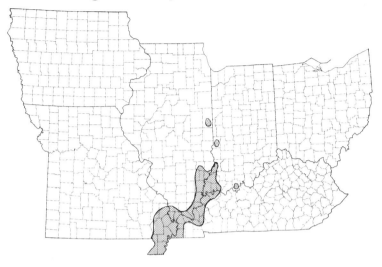

Atlas of United State Trees *Volume 1. Conifers and Important Hardwoods* by Elbert L. Little, Jr., Chief Dendrologist Division of Timber Management Research Miscellaneous Publication No. 1146

U.S. Department of Agriculture, March 1971 Forest Service, U.S. Government Printing Office Washington, D.C.

Natural range for Cucumber Tree

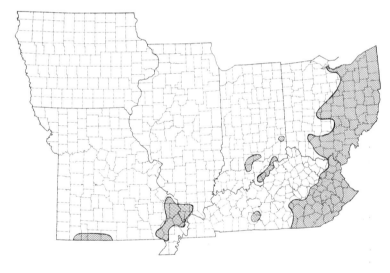

Atlas of United States Trees *Volume 1. Conifers and Important Hardwoods* by Elbert L. Little, Jr., Chief Dendrologist Division of Timber Management Research Miscellaneous Publication No. 1146

U.S. Department of Agriculture, March 1971 Forest Service, U.S. Government Printing Office Washington, D.C.

231

Natural range for Flowering Dogwood

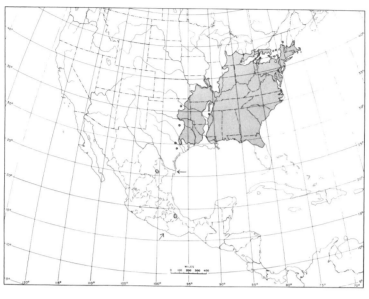

Silvics of Forest
Trees of the U.S.
Agriculture Hand-
book No. 271, 1965
U.S. Department of
Agriculture
Forest Service,
Washington, D.C.

Natural range for Black Gum

Silvics of Forest
Trees of the U.S.
Agriculture Hand-
book No. 271, 1965
U.S. Department of
Agriculture
Forest Service,
Washington, D.C.

Natural range for Sweet Gum

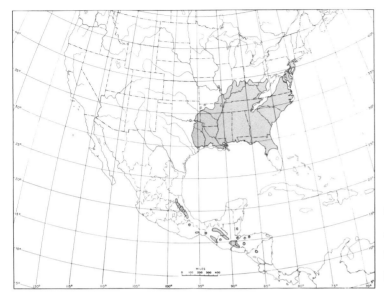

*Silvics of Forest
  Trees of the U.S.*
Agriculture Hand-
  book No. 271, 1965
U.S. Department of
  Agriculture
Forest Service,
  Washington, D.C.

Natural range for Hackberry

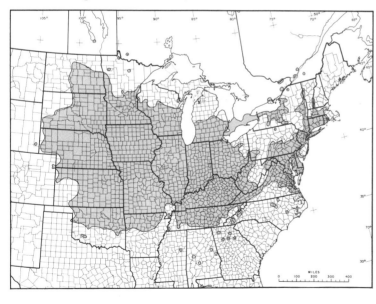

*Silvics of Forest
  Trees of the U.S.*
Agriculture Hand-
  book No. 271, 1965
U.S. Department of
  Agriculture
Forest Service,
  Washington, D.C.

233

Natural range for Mockernut Hickory

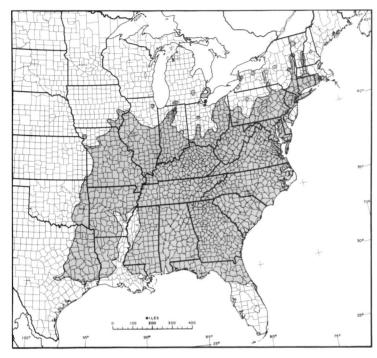

*Silvics of Forest
Trees of the U.S.*
Agriculture Hand-
book No. 271, 1965
U.S. Department of
Agriculture
Forest Service,
Washington, D.C.

Natural range for Pignut Hickory

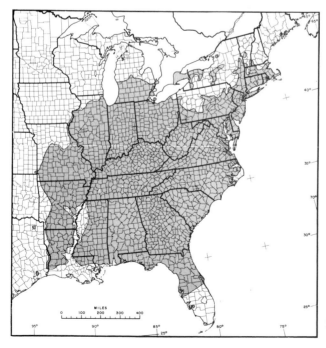

*Silvics of Forest
Trees of the U.S.*
Agriculture Hand-
book No. 271, 1965
U.S. Department of
Agriculture
Forest Service,
Washington, D.C.

Natural range for Shellbark Hickory

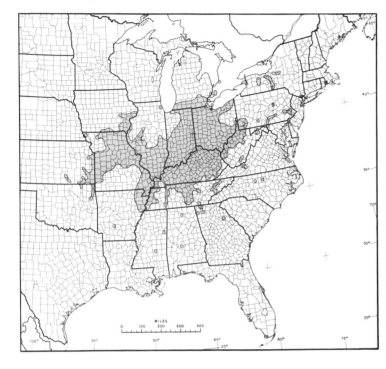

Silvics of Forest
  Trees of the U.S.
Agriculture Hand-
  book No. 271, 1965
U.S. Department of
  Agriculture
Forest Service,
  Washington, D.C.

Natural range for Black Locust

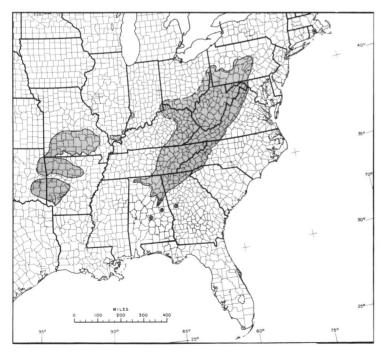

Silvics of Forest
  Trees of the U.S.
Agriculture Hand-
  book No. 271, 1965
U.S. Department of
  Agriculture
Forest Service,
  Washington, D.C.

235

APPENDIX

Natural range for Honey Locust

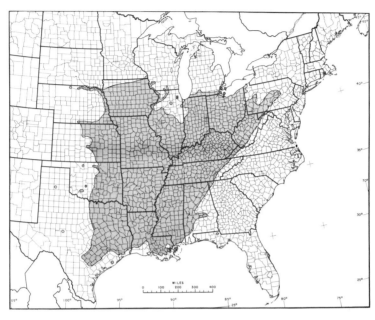

*Silvics of Forest
Trees of the U.S.*
Agriculture Hand-
book No. 271, 1965
U.S. Department of
Agriculture
Forest Service,
Washington, D.C.

Natural range for Red Maple

*Silvics of Forest
Trees of the U.S.*
Agriculture Hand-
book No. 271, 1965
U.S. Department of
Agriculture
Forest Service,
Washington, D.C.

236

Natural range for Osage Orange

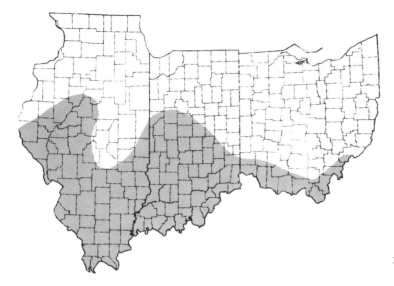

Map by Dwight
McCurdy

Natural range for Persimmon

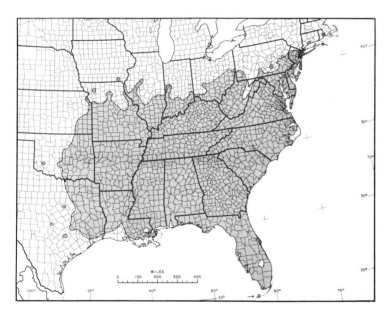

Silvics of Forest
   Trees of the U.S.
Agriculture Hand-
   book No. 271, 1965
U.S. Department of
   Agriculture
Forest Service,
   Washington, D.C.

237

APPENDIX

Natural range for Eastern White Pine

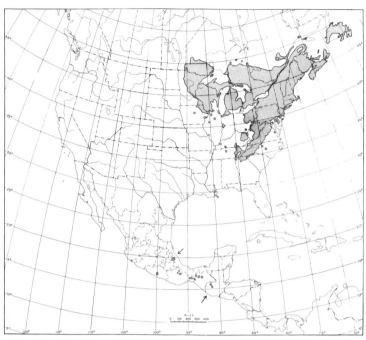

Silvics of Forest Trees of the U.S. Agriculture Handbook No. 271, 1965 U.S. Department of Agriculture Forest Service, Washington, D.C.

Natural range for Tulip Poplar

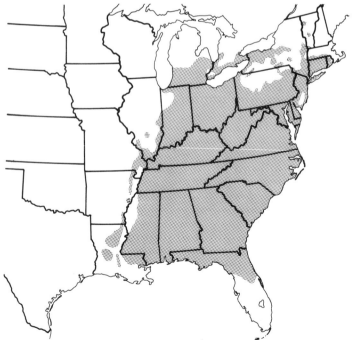

Silvics of Forest Trees of the U.S. Agriculture Handbook No. 271, 1965 U.S. Department of Agriculture Forest Service, Washington, D.C.

238

Natural range for Bur Oak

*Silvics of Forest
   Trees of the U.S.*
Agriculture Hand-
   book No. 271, 1965
U.S. Department of
   Agriculture
Forest Service,
   Washington, D.C.

Natural range for Chinkapin Oak

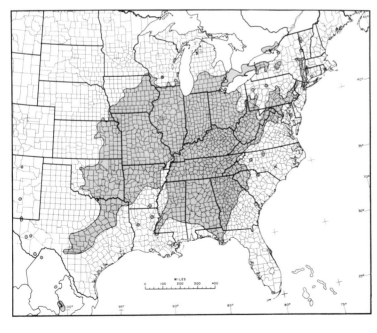

*Silvics of Forest
   Trees of the U.S.*
Agriculture Hand-
   book No. 271, 1965
U.S. Department of
   Agriculture
Forest Service,
   Washington, D.C.

239

APPENDIX

Natural range for Pin Oak

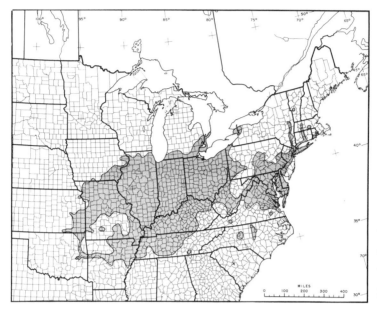

Silvics of Forest Trees of the U.S. Agriculture Handbook No. 271, 1965 U.S. Department of Agriculture Forest Service, Washington, D.C.

Natural range for Post Oak

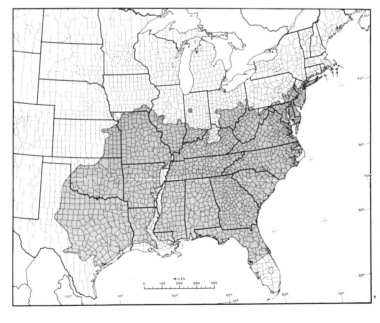

Silvics of Forest Trees of the U.S. Agriculture Handbook No. 271, 1965 U.S. Department of Agriculture Forest Service, Washington, D.C.

Natural range for Swamp White Oak

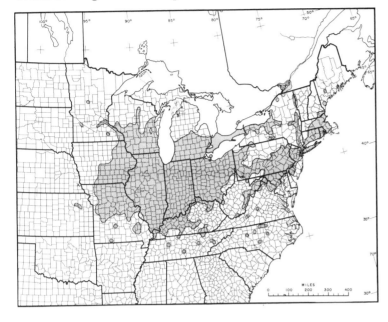

Silvics of Forest Trees of the U.S. Agriculture Handbook No. 271, 1965 U.S. Department of Agriculture Forest Service, Washington, D.C.

Natural range for Sassafras

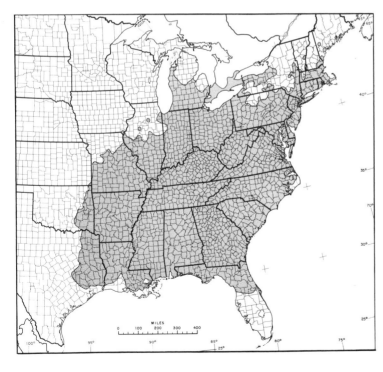

Silvics of Forest Trees of the U.S. Agriculture Handbook No. 271, 1965 U.S. Department of Agriculture Forest Service, Washington, D.C.

241

APPENDIX

Natural range for American Sycamore

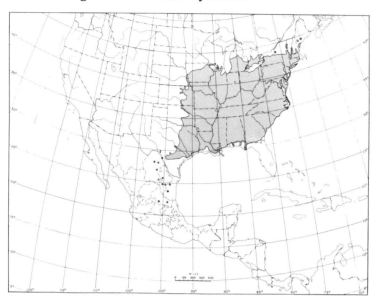

Silvics of Forest
Trees of the U.S.
Agriculture Hand-
book No. 271, 1965
U.S. Department of
Agriculture
Forest Service,
Washington, D.C.

242

Selected bibliography

Books

Anderson, Mark L. 1961. *The Selection of Tree Species*. Edinburgh and London: Oliver and Boyd.

Brockman, C. Frank. 1968. *Trees of North America*. New York: Golden Press.

Collingwood, G. H. and Warren D. Brush. 1963. *Knowing Your Trees*. Washington, D.C.: American Forestry Association.

Deam, Charles C. 1953. *Trees of Indiana*. 3rd rev. ed. Indianapolis: Bookwalter.

Enright, L. J. 1955. *Woody Plants for Landscape Use*. State College, Penn.: College Science Publishers.

Forbes, Reginald D. and Arthur B. Meyer, eds. 1961. *Forestry Handbook*. New York: Ronald Press.

Grimm, William Casey. 1957. *The Book of Trees*. Harrisburg, Penn.: Telegraph Press, Stackpole.

Harlow, William M. and Ellwood S. Harrar. 1958. *Textbook of Dendrology*. 4th ed. New York: McGraw-Hill.

Maino, Evelyn and Frances Howard. 1955. *Ornamental Trees*. Berkeley and Los Angeles: University of California Press.

Musser, H. Burton. 1962. *Turf Management*. New York, Toronto, London: McGraw-Hill, pp. 24–26.

Rehder, Alfred. 1934. *Manual of Cultivated Trees and Shrubs*. New York: Macmillan.

Sargent, Charles S. 1961. *Manual of the Trees of North America*. 2nd rev. ed., 2 vols. New York: Dover Publications.

Smith, David M. 1962. *The Practice of Silviculture*. 7th ed. New York, London, Sydney: John Wiley & Sons.

U.S., Department of Agriculture, Forest Service. 1948. *Woody Plant Seed Manual*. Miscellaneous Publication No. 654. Washington, D.C.: Government Printing Office.

————. 1965. *Silvics of Forest Trees in the United States*. Handbook No. 271. Washington, D.C.: Government Printing Office.

Articles

Carpenter, I. W. and A. T. Guard. 1954. Anatomy and morphology of the seedling roots of four species of the genus *Quercus*. *Journal of Forestry* 52: 269–74.

SELECTED BIBLIOGRAPHY

Fechner, G. H. 1951. Yellow-poplar lumber grade yield recovery—a guide to improved cutting. *Journal of Forestry* 49: 888–94.

Glascock, H. H., Jr. 1967. Foresters and environmental quality. *Journal of Forestry* 65: 378–80.

Green, William E. 1947. Effect of water impoundment on tree mortality and growth. *Journal of Forestry* 45: 118–20.

Hall, T. F. and G. E. Smith. 1955. Effects of flooding on woody plants, West Sands Development Project. *Journal of Forestry* 53: 281–85.

Klukas, Richard W. and Donald P. Duncan. 1967. Vegetational preference among Itasca Park visitors. *Journal of Forestry* 65: 18–21.

Rudolf, Paul O. 1967. Silviculture for recreation area management. *Journal of Forestry* 65: 385–90.

Thompson, Roger C. 1967. Preservation, recreation, and the premise of forestry. *Journal of Forestry* 65: 272–77.

Tocher, S. Ross, J. Alan Wager, and John D. Hunt. 1956. Sound management prevents worn out recreation sites. *Parks and Recreation.* March.

Pamphlets, bulletins, and circulars

Arnold Arboretum, Harvard University. 1936. *Bulletin of Popular Information.* Series 4, vol. 4, no. 14: 83–90.

Boyce, Stephen G. and David J. Neebe. 1959. *Trees for Planting on Strip-Mine Land in Illinois.* U.S. Forest Service, Central States Forest Experimental Station. Technical Paper No. 164.

Carter, J. Cedric. 1964. *Illinois Trees: Their Diseases.* Illinois Natural History Survey, Circular 46, pp. 1–93.

Chapman, A. G. 1967. *How Strip-Land Grading Affects Tree Survival and Growth.* Carbondale: Southern Illinois University, School of Agriculture Publication No. 29.

Finn, Raymond F. 1958. *Ten Years of Strip-Mine Forestation Research in Ohio.* U.S. Forest Service, Central States Forest Experimental Station. Technical Paper No. 153.

Illinois, Department of Conservation, Division of Forestry. 1955. *Forest Trees of Illinois.* Springfield: Illinois Department of Conservation.

Illinois Technical Forestry Association. 1965. *Recommended Silvicultural and Management Practices of Illinois Hardwood Forest Types.* Springfield: Illinois Technical Forestry Association.

Iowa State University of Science and Technology, Cooperative Extension Service. 1966. *Land-scape Plants for Iowa.*

Limstrom, G. A. and R. W. Merz. 1949. *Rehabilitation of Lands Stripped for Coal in Ohio.* U.S. Forest Service, Central States Forest Experimental Station. Technical Paper No. 113.

244

Scholz, Harold R. 1958. *Silvical Characteristics of American Basswood.* U.S. Forest Service, Lake States Forest Experimental Station. Station Paper No. 62.

U.S., Department of Agriculture. 1965. *The American Outdoors: Management for Beauty and Use.* Miscellaneous Publication No. 1000. Washington, D.C.: Government Printing Office.

————. 1966. *Trees for Shade and Beauty. Their Selection and Care.* Home and Garden Bulletin No. 117. Washington, D.C.: Government Printing Office.

————, Forest Service. 1935. Possibilities of Shelter-belt Planting in the Plains Region. Lake States Forest Experimental Station. Washington, D.C.: Government Printing Office.

Walker, Ernest D. and W. F. Purnell. 1964. *Understanding Soils.* Rev. ed. Urbana: University of Illinois, College of Agriculture, Cooperative Extension Service Circular 758.

Williston, H. L. 1959. *Inundation Damage to Upland Hardwoods.* U.S. Forest Service, Southern Forest Experimental Station, Southern Forest Notes No. 123.